Art Media Series

Creating with Crayons

Lothar Kampmann

 Van Nostrand Reinhold Company/New York

Illustrations

The work reproduced in the first part of this book is by students at the Dortmund branch of the Ruhr Pedagogical College, and by the author. That reproduced in the second part of the book, beginning on page 49, is taken from the collection of the Ruhr College Teacher Training Schools, and the Pelikan Archives. A few examples were also lent by the Karl-Rehbein School for Girls, in Hanau.
Sponsored by the Günther Wagner Pelikan-Werke, Hannover; and Koh-I-Noor, Inc., 100 North Street, Bloomsbury, New Jersey 08804

German edition © 1967
Otto Maier Verlag, Ravensburg, Germany.
Library of Congress Catalog Card Number 68-26803. ISBN 0-442-11321-8
Printed and bound in Germany
Published in the United States of America 1968 by Van Nostrand Reinhold Company,
450 West 33rd Street,
New York, N.Y. 10001.
A Division of Litton Educational Publishing, Inc.

16 15 14 13 12 11 10 9 8 7 6 5 4 3

Foreword

All children have an urge to draw, paint and model. They take great pleasure in it, and have an innate capacity for doing it well. This creative or constructive capacity is common to us all, imparted to us with life itself. We should do all we can to sustain and foster it by suitable means.

The child's urge to construct, his will to self-expression, plays an essential part in human development.

But the urge to construct will be atrophied if it is not cultivated and given an outlet in early youth, by the provision of materials: paper, paints and pencils. The child's first daubs and scribblings are so incomprehensible and meaningless to most adults, that many parents treat them as mere 'messes', prejudicial to cleanliness and tidiness. Every scrap of paper, every magazine, every book runs the risk of being scribbled over, often enough to the detriment of valuable possessions.

The new wallpaper gets painted on, or a valuable book, an important letter. But have we the right to find fault with the child? The child *must* paint, and will find opportunities to do so if none are provided. It has no appreciation of the adult's 'treasures'. In our children's interest we should pay more attention to cherishing the treasure of their creative capacity.

We must be sure of their always having some paper to paint on when they want it, even if it is only old bags and envelopes, or the cheapest typing paper. When they are a little older and more sensible, they should have a drawing-block 'all to themselves'. On it they are 'free' to paint—this is very important. Certain not to be scolded, they will have their work praised. Praise is as important to the child's soul as food is to the body. The child's creative urge will be frightened out of him only too soon if he is forever discovering that painting is forbidden, here, there and everywhere. Especially if he is proudly preparing to show a new picture to his parents—a picture which, unfortunately, was done on something of great value to them. Punishment convinces the child that painting is something wrong, that one would be better off to avoid it altogether. But in his scribbling and daubing the child is putting down his ideas of a world that exists, first of all, for himself alone. He is putting down his relationship to the world, to its

3

pleasures and pains. By doing so he sets himself free, objectifying his contact with the still incomprehensible adult world. He creates his own objects, which signify that world to him, expressing through them his connections with the world, and creating new ones for himself in so doing.

To make a mark on paper, the child will grab the first thing that comes to hand. Nowadays this is usually a ballpoint pen, which soon cramps a child's hand with its hard stroke—a stroke, moreover, without any character, having always the same thickness, and incapable of expressing anything. A pencil would be far better, especially a soft one. But the pencil has only one colour, an 'unchildish' black. Art educators and industry have together created the wax crayon, which has all the qualities of the pencil, yet allows the child to scribble around on the paper, producing bold strokes, with the additional advantage of colour. Crayons can be used in all sorts of ways, and form an ideal medium. This book on wax crayon techniques is intended to interest and stimulate work with them in the home as well as in school.

Techniques for working with wax crayons

No child is too small to use wax crayons. They are so easy to hold that the youngest child can handle them. They can produce lively pictures, as well as the dots, tentatively evolved shapes, and symbols to which children give variable meanings—to the adult, signs from another world, to which he no longer has access.

These paintings are vitally important to the child. Through them he can take a significant step forward in the world; they are outward signs of his own small, self-enclosed personality.

The wax crayon might be called the predestined tool for this motorized psychical unburdening. It will not crumble, splinter or break off as easily as most pencils, because of the flexible wax in its composition. The child is not threatened by the real danger of a sharply pointed pencil, and the picture will not become blurred under his hand.

Wax crayons will 'paint' on any surface—paper, wood, cardboard, glass, metal or plastics. Modern plastic-top tables plainly demand to be painted on. They will suffer no harm from wax crayons, which can easily be wiped off with detergent or turpentine substitute.

A nursery door, the surface of which has been coated with plastic paint, makes an ideal 'blackboard' for the child to paint on with crayons. There will be no chalk dust on the floor, and the child can paint 'on the wall' to his heart's content.

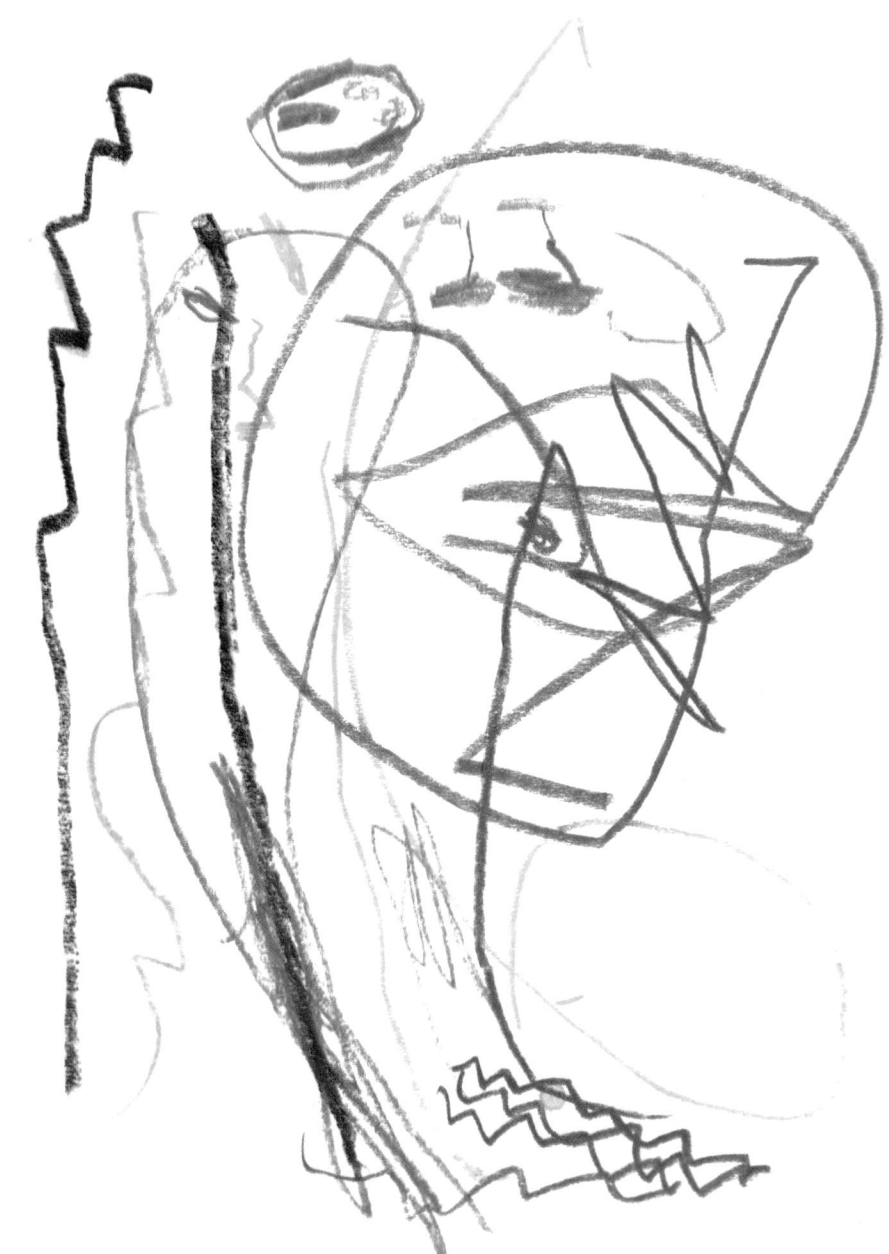

What pencil could produce such rich, colourful strokes as these? The thick stroke is an inspiration in itself, inviting the user to work more boldly than with a pointed pencil; on a larger scale and over a much larger area. This frees a dynamic force. The wider swing is a release to the child, liberating him inwardly.

Quite early, the right hand becomes accustomed to doing all essential jobs, while the left hand remains culpably neglected. Wax crayons, working so well and easily over a surface, are particularly suitable for ambidextrous painting. Children can even work with both hands at once. You can say, for instance, 'Let's knead the dough. First with one hand, then with the other, and then with both together.' (Attach the paper or the drawing-pad to the table with adhesive tape, to prevent it from slipping.)

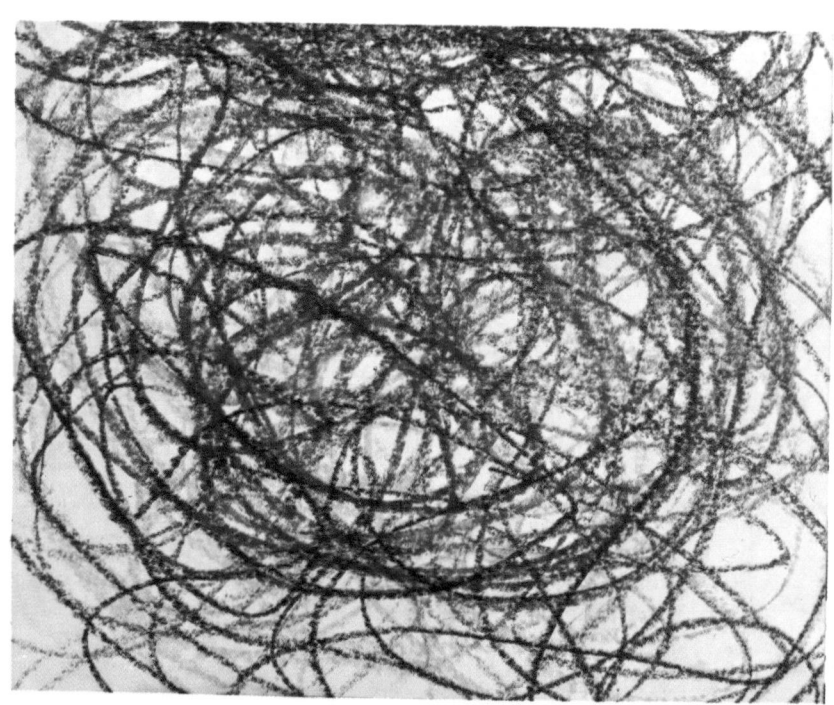

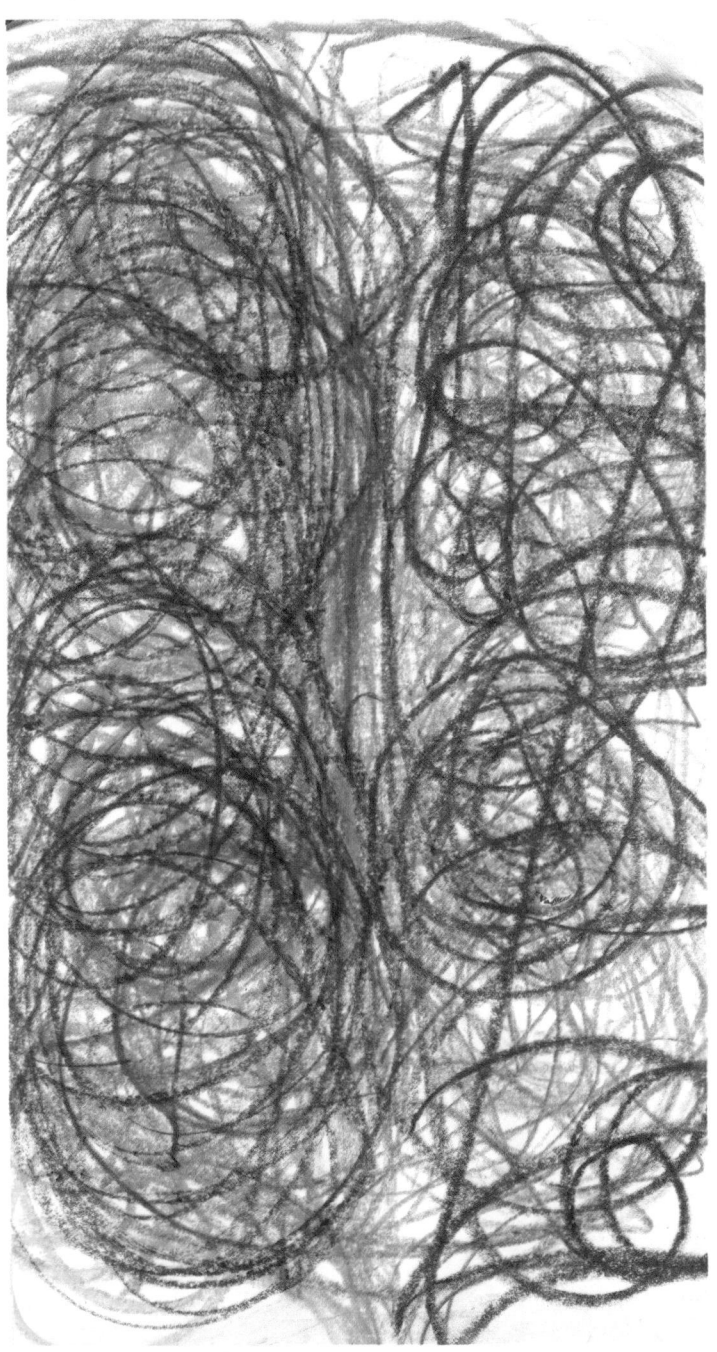

When at first children see only their own vital energy 'rotating' in colour on the paper, it will surely encourage them to use a lot of colours, and paint larger, more colourful pictures. As they get older they will see to it that the picture they have in mind really evolves. Every child will paint according to his own temperament.

It is exciting for the child to discover the different effects which the picture can be made to convey by the use of many colours. They will learn a lot by painting on different papers. The paper should not always be white. Coloured papers can greatly help to foster the child's urge to self-expression, without demanding too much of his intelligence by the need for a difficult technique.

9

'Town at twilight', particularly effective on grey paper,

or the farmer ploughing, on brown paper. These coloured papers can be bought, but they can just as well be hand-made with opaque paint, with the added advantage that one can obtain the exact shade of colour desired.

Wax colours stand out particularly brightly on black paper. The coloured lanterns in the holiday procession look quite real and festive here,

snowflakes, too, with their wonderful crystalline shapes,

or a glittering array of precious stones.

A wax crayon does without difficulty what no ordinary pencil can: it covers a surface in broad stretches, as brilliantly as the thickest opaque paints, when rubbed on the paper with a strong, even pressure. All this without the risk of splashing colour or spilled water.

The flowers glow as if painted with heavy oil colours.

On the other hand, a gentle pressure will give an impression of delicate pastel painting.

Further details of the qualities and technical possibilities, leading to new forms of composition.

All dark wax crayons contain a greater proportion of wax, and therefore are softer. This means that they can be painted or drawn over a light-coloured wax-crayon ground. Dark colours are opaque.

13

Yellow over blue = green

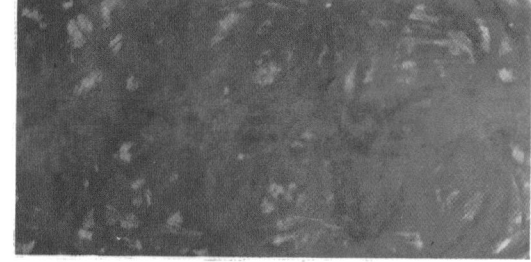

Yellow over red = orange

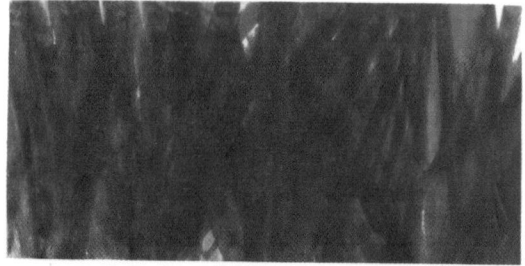

Red over blue = violet

White over black = grey

The lighter colours are naturally harder, having less wax and more colour content. They are not opaque when laid on a dark ground but stir it up and produce a mixture of colours. Of course there is a wide range of other combinations to be worked out by individual experimentation.

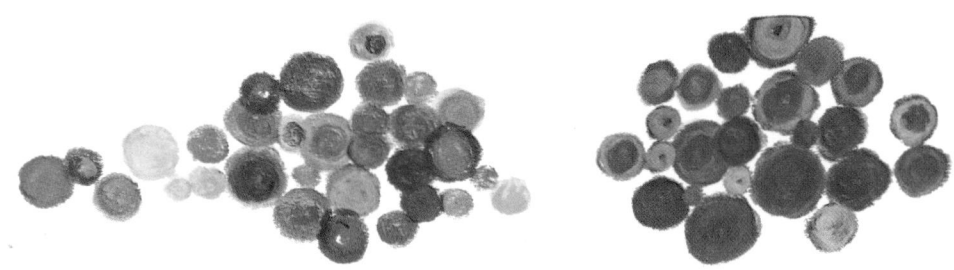

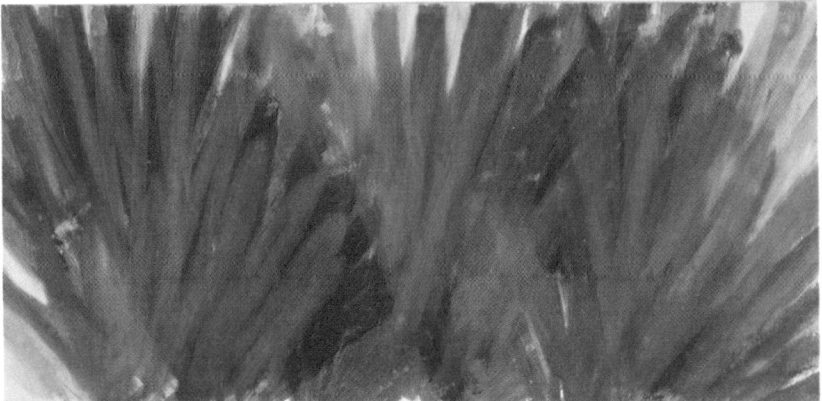

Having learnt both how to mix them and how to apply them thickly, we can now start actual 'painting' with these crayons. We shall get different results, however, according to whether we paint on rough, smooth or a shiny 'art' paper. On rough paper the strokes will not fill the surface as thickly, and thus the colours will mix more thoroughly, while the picture retains more of a chalky character.

15

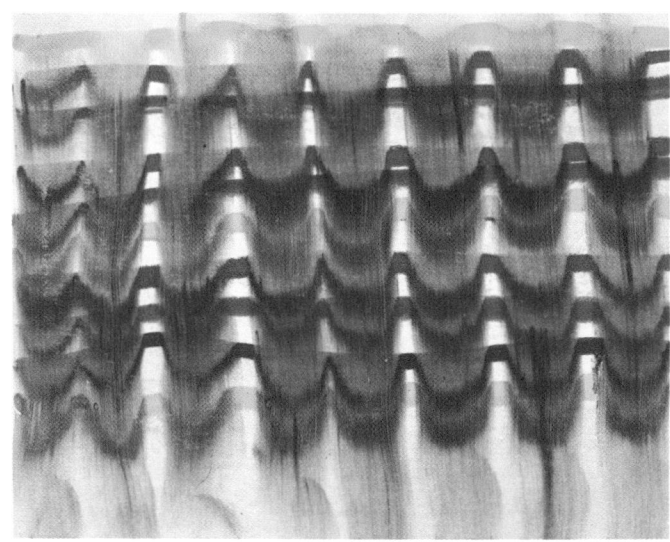

On entirely smooth art paper, the crayons can be rubbed and mixed with the fingers or with a paint rag.

Backgrounds can be prepared in delicate tones such as this, and then painted over with strong colours.

As we have said, light colours can be covered with dark ones, because the soft, dark ones will not disturb the harder, light ones. Black is the softest colour of all, and the most opaque.

If we fill a sheet of paper with bright colours

like this

or this

or even quite differently, (but always applying the colours firmly and thickly), and then cover it all with a layer of soft black, this layer can be removed from the coloured ground with any sharp-edged object. The colours will then reappear. This technique is called 'sgraffito', 'scraper-painting' or 'scratch-drawing'.

19

1. Scratched with the point only.
2. Strong, broad outlines.

3. Surface scraped away, leaving black outlines for emphasis.

1   2   3

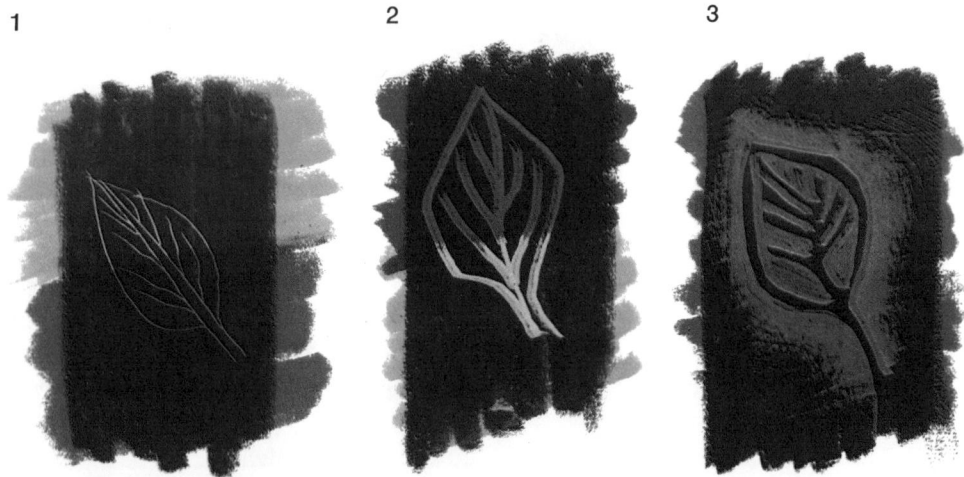

'Sgraffito' becomes most interesting and expressive, of course, when all these possibilities are combined.

Anything that can be done with a black overlay can, of course, be done with other dark colours. They will give the painting a completely fresh colour effect, which in turn will determine and support other forms of composition. When practising this 'scraper art', children are apt to forget that the soft, scraped-off crayon will collect at the edges of the drawing and on the table. Before long this will be clinging to their clothes or will have fallen on the floor, to be rubbed or trodden in. Children tend simply to blow the crumbs away from the paper, thus it is advisable to spread a good-sized underlay of newspaper or cardboard on the table, on which the

crumbs will do no harm. A similar 'scraper-picture' effect can be obtained by painting over the wax ground with casein colour, which, unlike light-coloured wax crayons, can easily cover up dark colours, presenting fresh technical possibilities. The usual method is to let the layer of paint dry on the wax ground with casein colours, which, wherever it happens to have been painted on more thickly, producing an effect that has a charm of its own. But there is no need to wait for the paint to dry. The work can be done rapidly with the handle of a paintbrush or with a strip of cardboard while the colour is still wet.

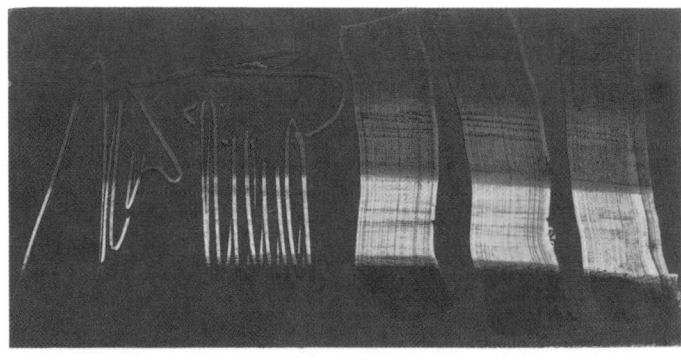

Work done with paintbrush handle and the edge of a cardboard strip.

Quite painterly effects are obtained by partially wiping out the wet layer of colour with a rag.

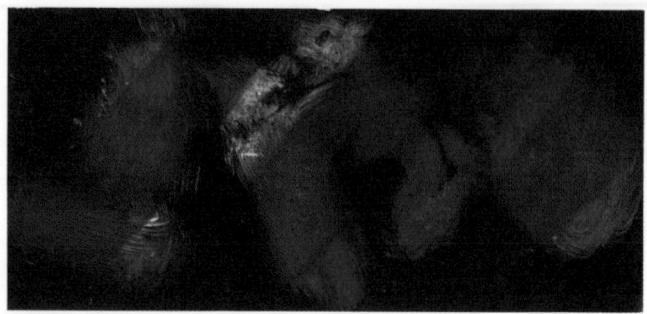

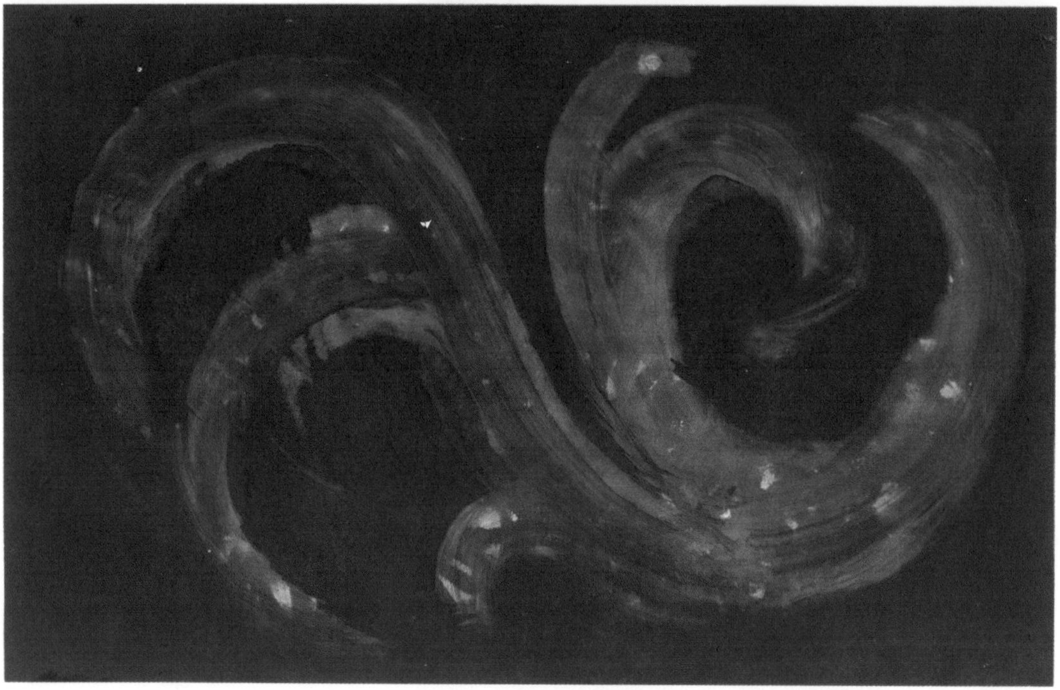

The wax ground can also be coated with black Chinese ink, though this demands some patience, as the ink is apt to run together into little drops on the wax. It must always be used undiluted, with a very wide brush and applied repeatedly until the paper is covered with an unbroken film of black.

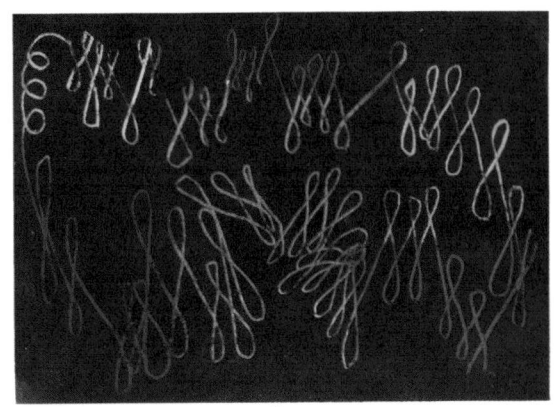

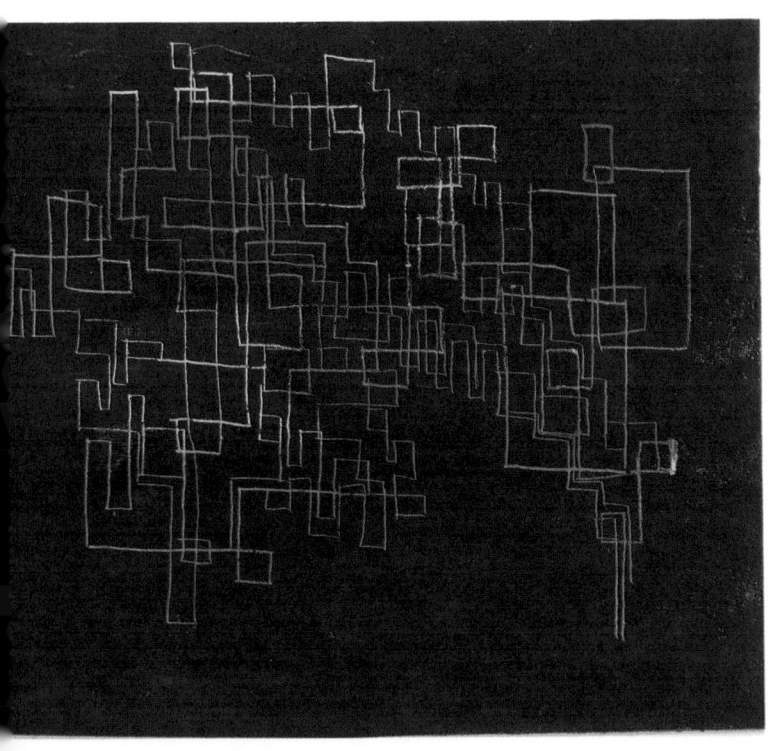

You can scratch and scrape into this ground as well as on the wax-crayon layer below. The wax underneath must, however, be absolutely compact and thick, otherwise the watery ink will seep through wherever it is not water-tight; producing black marks which cannot be removed.

This ink covering has a peculiar charm, because black though it is, it is transparent. The child can see his picture underneath, which makes it easier for him to scrape out certain colours. But there are other difficulties to contend with. Besides the danger of getting thoroughly dirty, there is a dis-advantage in that the ink takes some time to dry, and the paper warps meanwhile. For this reason, the paper should be fastened to the board until it is dry.

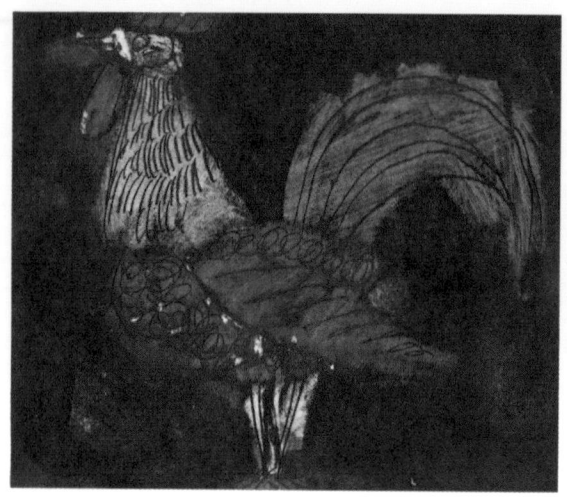

It is astonishing what a lot of things one can do with wax crayons. For instance, ink and wax resistant etching.

For this, the paper must be partly or entirely coated with the crayon. This coating is then 'etched' or scratched with a needle after being polished with a soft cloth. A brush, full of ink, is then drawn over the design, taking care to see that the lines get thoroughly filled with ink.

When the ink is dry, the whole sheet is carefully scraped with the blade of a knife.

The wax coating has prevented the ink from penetrating to the paper except through the scratched lines.

26

On the same principle, that wax repels water, a combined wax crayon and water-colour technique can be employed.

Where the paper is not protected by the wax it will absorb the water-colour. Quite impressive paintings can be produced with soft wax crayon, if a simple drawing on white paper is 'transfigured' by bright colours.

Light wax colours can have darker water-colours painted over them. But it is just as easy, really, to paint light water-colours over dark ones. In both cases the paint must be watery, not opaque.

This technique resembles Batik, and is often called 'paper Batik'. This water-colour process can of course be carried out with diluted black Chinese ink, painted rapidly over the wax, but it will detach itself from the wax in tiny drops.

Again variations are possible here. If the picture, painted over with Chinese ink as described above, is washed under the water tap, a general grey tone will result. After thorough drying, further paintings can be done over this, coated for protection, and then washed clear.

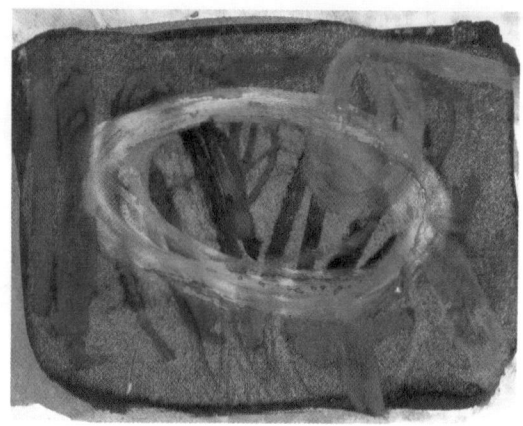

Coloured inks are very suitable for this 'Batik' work, producing pictures of the greatest brilliance.

We can also combine black and coloured inks. Cover the paper with black ink, wash it off, dry the paper, then go on painting with especially bright colours, and finish off with coloured inks.

Wax crayons have another important characteristic: they are soluble in turpentine and benzine.
A painting done in heavy strokes of colour can be blurred with a paintbrush dipped in turpentine, to produce outstanding 'painterly' effects.

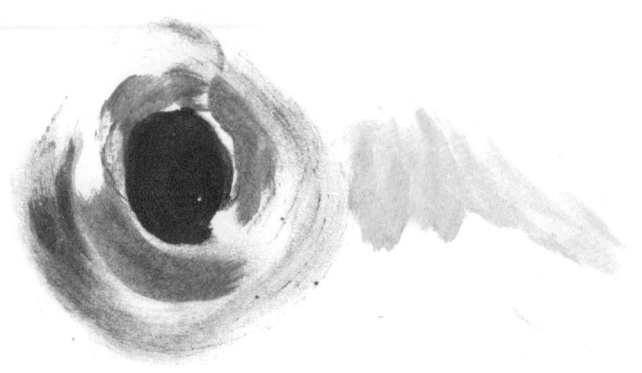

Wax-crayon compositions can be blurred in this way with a finger, or even a rag dipped in turpentine, and then worked over afterwards in wide areas or lines.

We can take advantage of the solubility of wax crayons to practise the technique seen here. Large forms can be washed out of a crayoned background with turpentine.

Rag and paintbrush were both used to wash out here. Further colour and outlines were added in crayon afterwards.

Painting can, of course, be done with pre-dissolved crayon and brush, producing the effect of glazed water-colour or oil-colour techniques.

If a sheet of paper is soaked in turpentine and laid over a painting in thick wax crayon, then pressed or rubbed, a mirror image of the original, in delicate pastel tones, will result.

A multiple method of reproduction can be evolved from this if the original is painted on fine sandpaper, which tends to retain the wax colour. The 'prints' can then be used further to form a whole series.

This last technique might be termed a printing process. The sandpaper retains at least enough wax for about five or six pulls. The pattern 'block' can then be very easily refilled with colour.

Everyone knows what can be done with carbon paper. Put a sheet of it, coloured side upwards, under a plain sheet of paper, and draw. You get a print that is reversed, and of a deep black. Place the carbon paper on top, carbon side down, and your drawing is as black as before, but right way around.

And now another 'printing process', facilitated by the consistency of the wax crayon, and best carried out with the darker shades since they are softer.
Instead of carbon paper, take a sheet of drawing board, cover it thickly with crayon, and proceed as above, but use greater pressure.

There is another 'printing process', known to us from childhood. We used to place a coin under a piece of paper and take a rubbing from it with a pencil. This can also be done with a wax crayon.

And if we look about us we can find a lot of other things to treat in the same way.

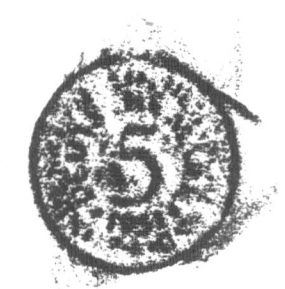

This little lace pattern can produce a lot of copies if we shift the paper; and we can even vary the crayon colour. Large surfaces can be covered in this way.

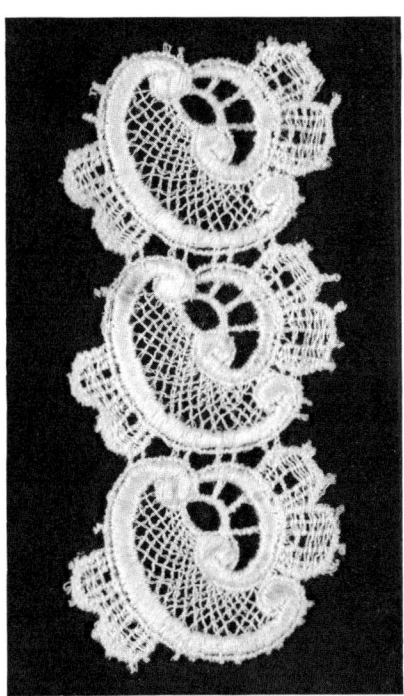

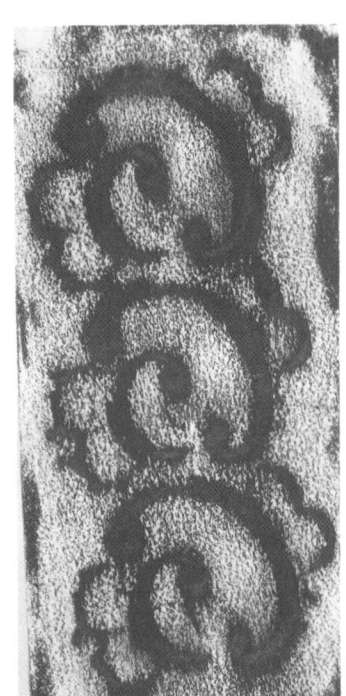

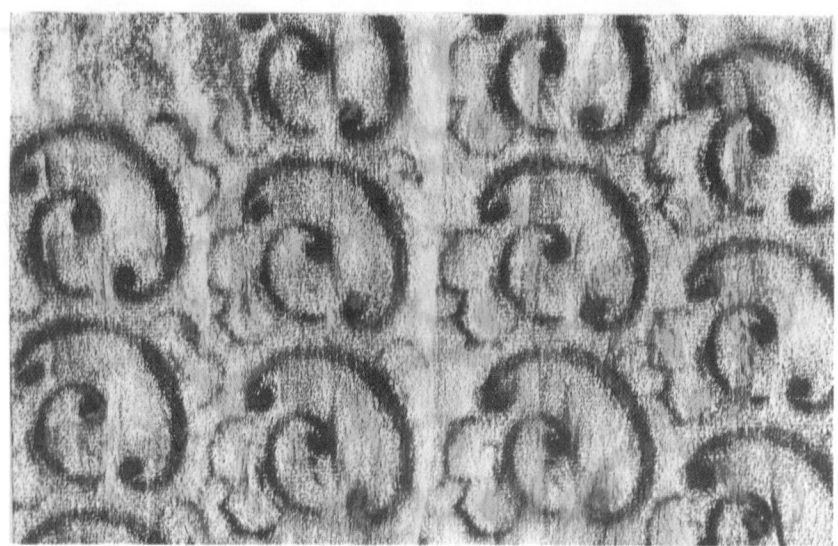

In the example below, textured cut-glass was used as an underlay. One can also experiment with rubbed patterns of strong-ribbed leaves, and grasses.

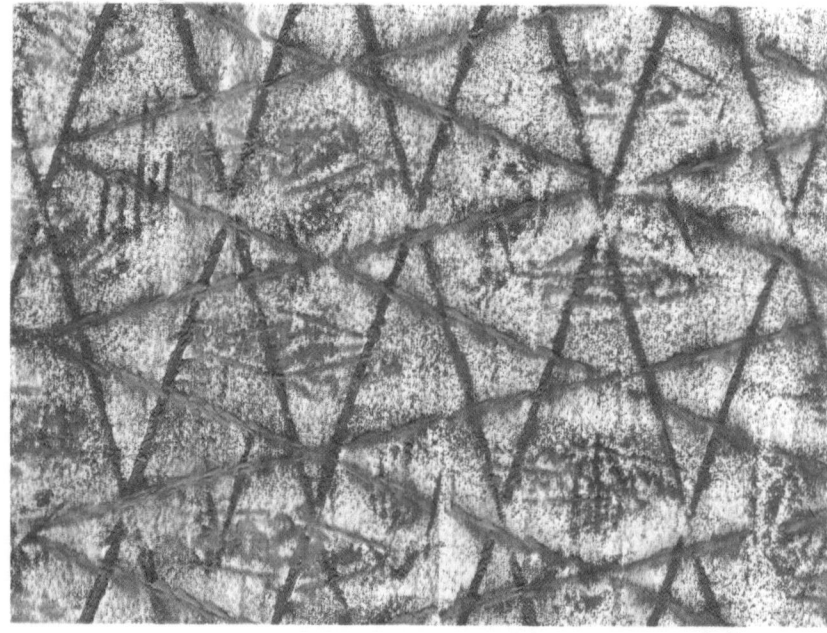

Skilfully composed, rubbings of this kind can be used to make pictorial designs. The simplest way of producing rubbed linear motifs is to glue down pieces of string or cord.

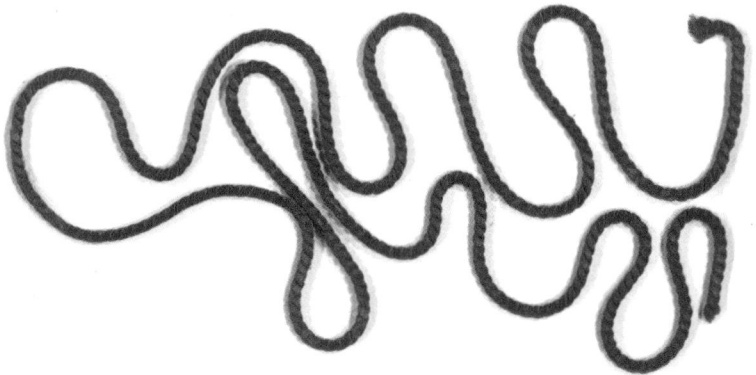

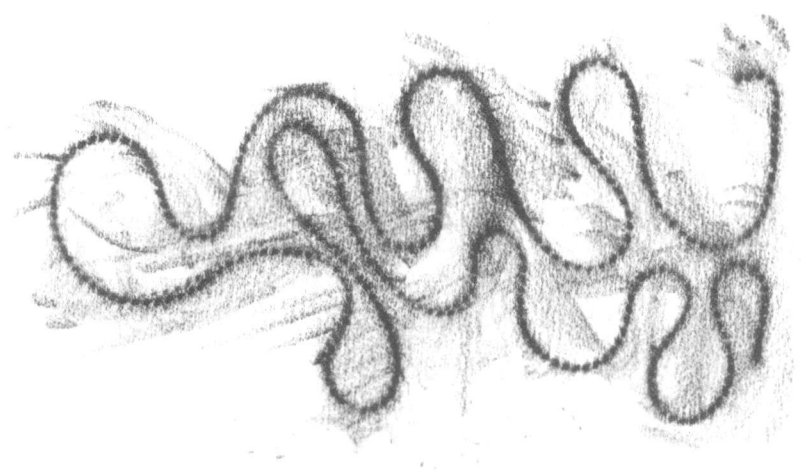

And finally, we have one more technique, which should really have been described at the beginning. This is the 'encaustic' process of early western painting. Pastes made of wax and powdered pigment were applied with a spatula

to the plaster covering of the wall. The colour was melted into the dry, absorbent plaster by holding red-hot metal plates in front of it. This is how paintings of the golden age of Pompeiii have come down to us in undiminished beauty. The essential factor in all encaustic is that the coloured wax be melted under the influence of heat. This can be done in various ways, two of which, given proper preparation, are practicable even in school.

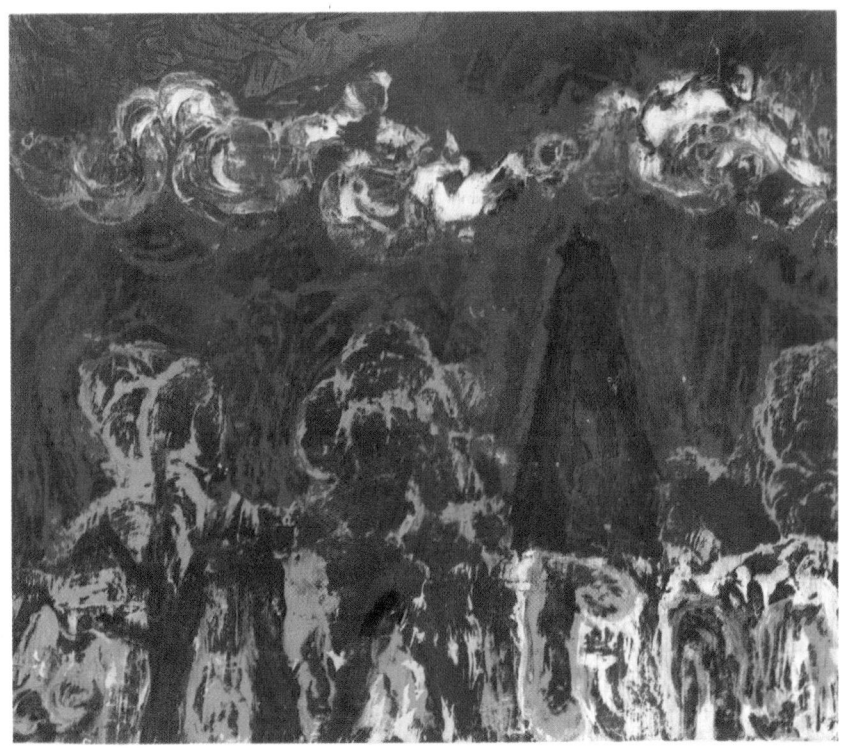

Both at school and at home, however, walls must be spared; so here is another, more practicable method, based on the same principle. The implement for the purpose is the electric hair-drier. This is used to heat the paper ,while the drawing is actually being done on the hot surface. As the wax crayon melts, it covers the paper with a thick, uneven layer of colour; an unusual form of painting in itself.

If a blow-lamp is available, or a large sheet of metal can be heated by some other means, the paper can be laid on the hot sheet and painted. Both methods have their advantages and disadvantages. One can easily burn one's fingers and the paper on the hot sheet, but one can paint unrestrictedly on every part of the paper. Handling the hair-drier and painting at the same time is a complicated business and needs great attention, but there is no danger of burning oneself or the paper.

Pictures of this kind can have additional tempera colour rubbed over them with the thumb, and when the paint is dry the entire picture can be smoothed with a piece of glass or a scissors blade. Flakes of paint will be left in the furrows, and if the wax crayon is applied with a heated spatula, the effect will be like that of an oil painting.

Examples of students' work

The versatility of wax crayons is really quite astonishing. Whatever the degree of technical skill or pictorial talent of the user, crayons will always prove to be a very satisfactory means of self-expression. The art teacher is well-advised to experiment with them —there will always be some fresh possibility for him to discover.

In the following section, the students' work reproduced will show the ways in which wax crayons can be effectively used.

What cultural inheritance is most likely to stimulate a child's creative urge? Everything that may encourage the invention of stories and fables. All the fairy-tale happenings the child thinks of as taking place in unusual surroundings, in which animals, plants and buildings are all of a strange kind, in fabulous forms and colours. Fairy tales and sagas offer them much imaginative materials, and yet it is dismaying to see how lacking in fantasy children prove to be when asked to picture scenes from a tale they have been told. This is almost certainly due to the way in which the material is presented to them. It is asking too much of a child, to say to him, 'Now think of a lovely picture to make out of this story'. There will be so many pictorially interesting scenes to choose from, that they need to be discussed.

The mistake is usually made of treating this material only as literature, so that the pictorial side is less emphasised than the linguistic and mental. But the art teacher can enlarge on it and talk about the splendid lamps, the strange shapes of the trees, the wonderful colours of the walls, and the extraordinary shapes of castles and dragons.

Thus we see that it is not enough to say 'Today we'll paint a magical bird'. The children will want to invent things about it first. Each of them can think of finer feathers, stranger wings, eyes and beak, to enlighten the others about the wondrous appearance of this bird. The next theme might then be taken from the particular real world surrounding them, inviting consideration, observation and pictorialising.

Country children have different surroundings from those of city-dwellers; quiet children's differ from those of adventurous ones. It must not be supposed that all the visual phenomena in a child's surroundings automatically become a part of his personal world. They are only integrated into it if the child has had some personal contact with them as part of his experience. This does not mean, however, that the child will then paint any of these phenomena—fish, tree, basket, apple, mouse or cow—'better', more 'true to nature', more 'correctly'. He has captured it for ever in his own symbols, out of his inner fund of experience, which allows him to fill these signs with his personal life. Anything unrelated to his own life will be drawn in stiff, indifferent symbols. Formative association with objects helps the child in his efforts to relate to his surrounding world, while developing his ability to see consciously and constructively, to co-ordinate eye, touch and sensation with thought and action. Through his own movements he discovers the need of functional reactions.

We can arrange a number of objects beside one another to form a 'still life', but we are thinking of the environment of the child as we come to our third basic theme, the combined appearance of the natural and the man-made world around him, if only in partial aspects. Here again it is not enough to say 'We'll paint a landscape', or 'a town'. We must, as before, make real contact with the subject. Pictures of home life are in their place here, as are those of adult working life, as far as the children are concerned with it. Subjects like 'our street', 'our town', 'the factory district at the edge of the town', or 'traffic incidents'.

None of these subjects is intended for any special technique, but one particular technique may represent the most expressive medium for some definite purpose.

A town in the darkness of night—the lights have just been turned on, and the windows glow in the dark houses. This scene can be most impressively represented by a wax scraper picture. The lamps actually light up one after another in the black paint, the windows shine out, the outlines of the houses become faintly visible.

Or the bare, black winter forest, becoming visible again after the snowstorm. The paper, blackened with wax crayon, is coated with casein white, and the scraper allows us to 'rediscover' the trees under snow.

For 'amusing' subjects, direct techniques are best. Whatever we draw or paint with wax crayons will be graphic elements—lines or dots, small or large flat areas. And the colours will be there—red, blue and yellow, with those that derive from these primary colours, plus black and white. Out of all these, and our knowledge of the material, we can invent subjects.

All flat or spatial design is an arrangement of constructive elements. Here we have them simplified. Instead of 'A big red ball on a long black beam', we say 'A great, round red over a long, black horizontal'.

There are many ways of motivating tasks of this kind, and we must go about it differently with small children than with their seniors. For example, the subject may be complementary colouring, and we leave it to their choice whether the combination is to be red and green, blue and orange or violet and yellow. One of the colours in the composition is to be constantly active. It can take the form of a line, a dot or a surface, but always an elementary one. There are many ways of setting the task:

1. A formation of red dots forces its way into an arrangement of green ones.
2. One or several orange lines go astray, reassemble, and disperse again among a tangle of blue spots of different shapes.
3. We look down on a large forest, through which Red Indians are ranging.
4. We arrange oranges on a blue tablecloth.
5. Heavy violet lines are attacked by little, nimble, yellow ones.

Every art teacher is constantly faced with the task of encouraging his pupils to paint by suggesting suitable subjects. Giving a pupil a theme sets him on his way; he has been challenged to prove his capacity.

It could be said that the whole world is at one's command to provide subjects for art teaching; but much of it is only attractive in theory, or to adult eyes, while the child feels no connection with it. And many subjects have little use in art education.

Thus, the educational content of

what we offer the child must be examined for its pictorial significance, and even then not all of these will prove to be an absolute stimulus to production. It must suit the child, and he must have some integral relationship to it. We cannot simply say 'Paint this or that'. Our themes must be derived from the two facets of art education, which should always be considered together: the legitimate desire of the children, according to their needs, and the educational duty of the teacher, as trustee, both to the children and to society at large.

p. 47, above:
'Rhythmic curves, suggesting handwriting'. Curve and rhythm, such as we need in script. The subject given was to do an imaginary letter, written part narrowly, part broadly.

p. 47, below:
The curves were drawn rhythmetically on a black background.

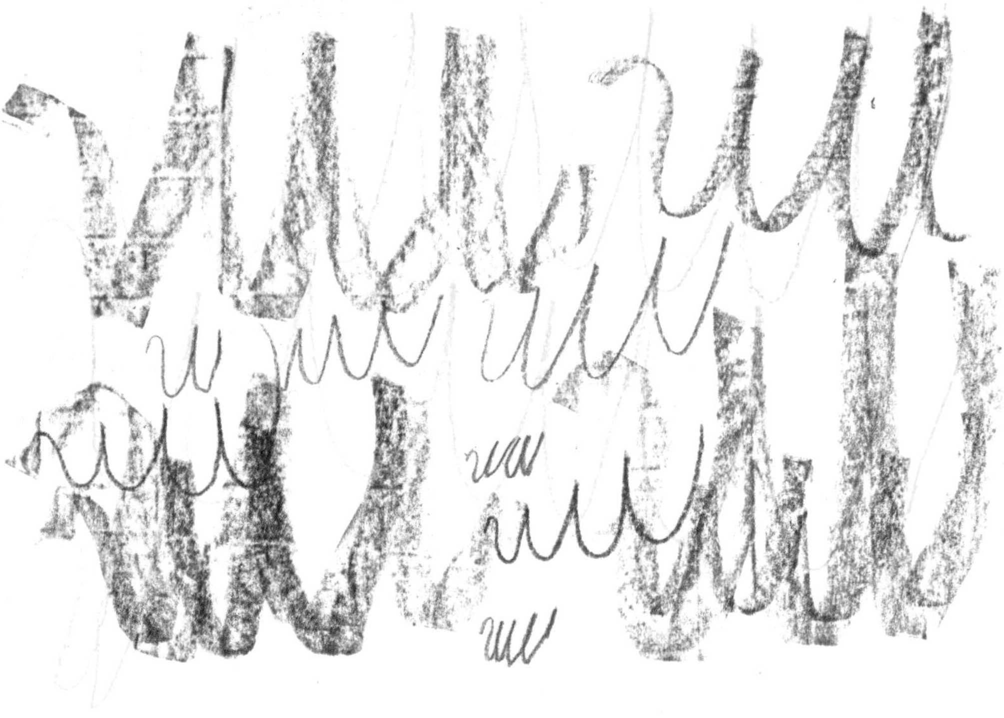

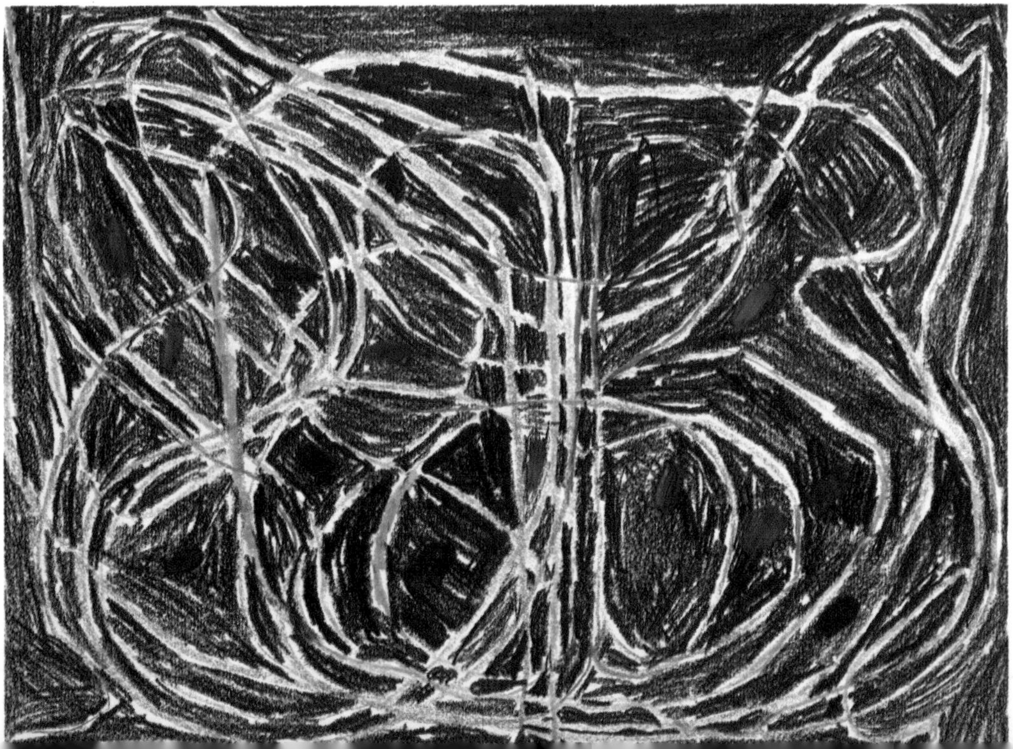

After the uncontrolled, now the rhythmic. Lines in an undulating rhythm, winding horizontally over one another. Worked over with paintbrush and turpentine.

After the wavy line, the rectangularly varied one, overlapping the one before it. These interstices, like the former, demand to be filled in. Worked over with turpentine.

48

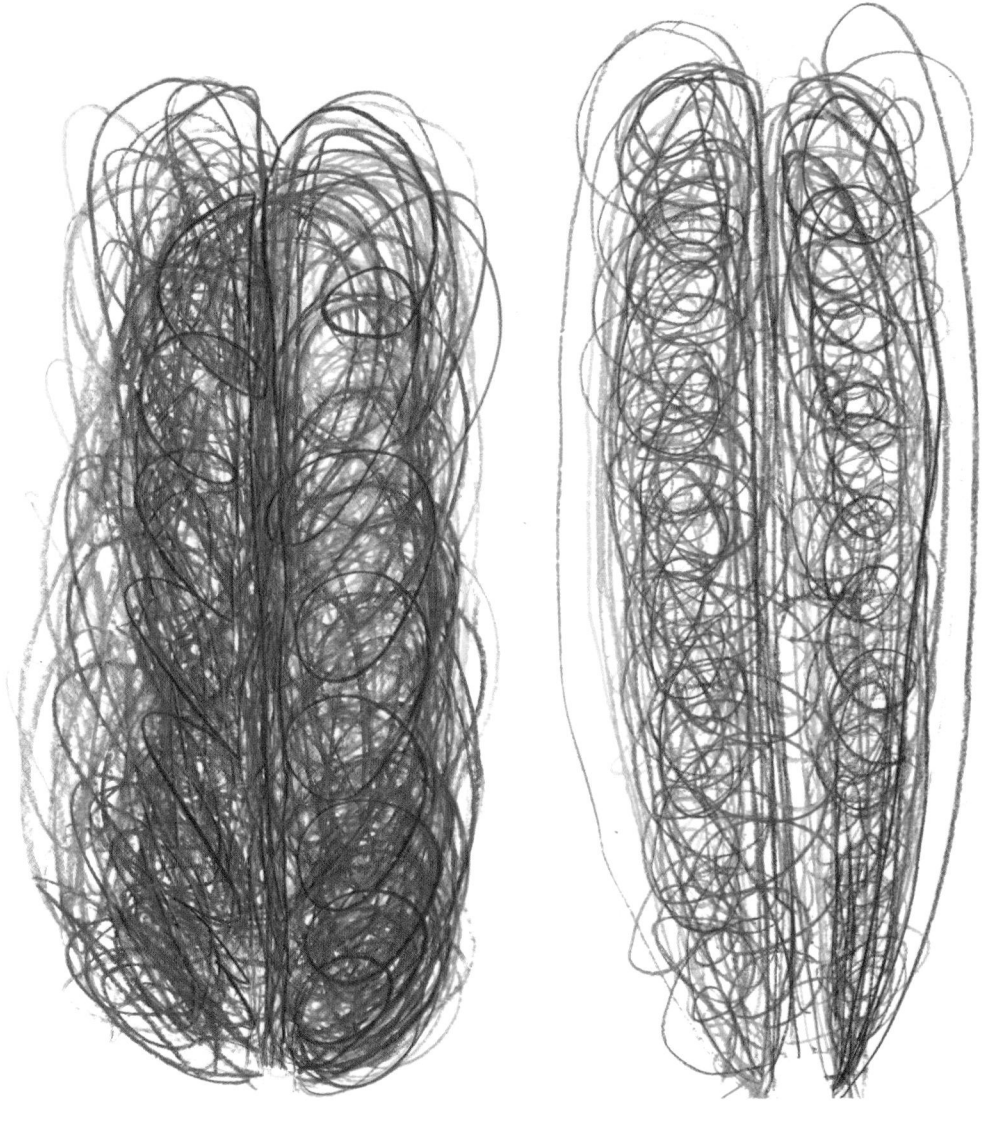

'Ambidextrous exercises in curves.'
It is interesting to see how each
child will work with a different
motor impulse.

Pupils can do more than one
thinks. The task was 'Paint the big
trees in the forest'. For technique,
see p. 12.

From the story of Hansel and Gretel. The picture shows clearly how the child makes a static line-up of this most dynamic story. For technique, see p. 12.

51

'Little beetles have flown to the big flower and settled down on it.' For technique, see p. 12.

'Bathing.' Painted in patches with wax crayons (boy, 11). For technique, see p. 12.

The tale of Aladdin and the wonderful lamp, which is full of pictures.

This is the 'Flight of the Carpet', seen pictorially. The child was faced with a real picture this time: he sees the carpet flying high in the air; under it lie houses, roads, lakes, hills and woods. The boy (9) has so identified himself with the picture that his oriental road has unexpectedly become a modern highway with a lot of bright-coloured cars.

'The giant's playthings' (girl, 8).
For technique, see p. 12.

'Football' (girl, 14). The wax
crayons were laid on very thick.
For technique, see p. 41.

'Rooster.' This large, bright figure
was painted by a girl during her
first schooldays. It is amusing to
see the unconcern with which she
had given it three legs and a
human face.

'An evening walk in the forest.' For
technique, see p. 12.

'The Ship.' Painted with wax
crayons in a simple technique. For
technique, see p. 12.

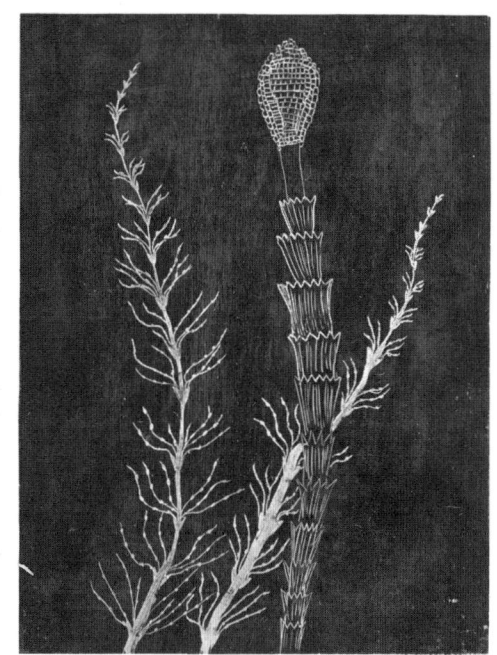

'Horsetail.' Nature study. The ground was laid in white crayon and then covered with black. For technique, see p. 23.

These trees were 'scraped'. Black tempera had been painted over the yellow wax background. Each of the four children has a different idea of a tree and its growth.

They used their scraper as they would a pencil, drawing lines even where they really wanted a space effect. They were not yet accustomed to the new technique, the tools, or the way to use them.

It would have been a good idea to introduce them to this technique in a sort of game, like this: 'Let's look at our scraper. You've all done some scraping with the fine point, which makes very fine, delicate strokes, the kind we want for delicate, thin branches. But there are other ends to the scraper,

with which you can make medium thick, and even very thick lines. And with the side you can scrape out whole patches. Now let's imagine we're flying over a big town. There are big, wide streets in it (for the side of the scraper), and medium wide streets (for the medium scraper), and little, narrow ones (for the point of the scraper), and of course a big square that we can scratch out with the full side of the scraper. And now we can make a map of the whole town.

We can see the same sort of thing in a feather, which has a stout quill with finer and finer barbs springing out of it.

We can see it too in the veins of leaves, which give us a good subject for using our scraper.

Or the vine, which has both wavy lines and broad patches to show.

This picture, 'Swimming', was done by a girl of 14 in the sgraffito technique on a white wax ground. For technique, see pp. 20 and 22.

'A dark town.' Coated with casein and then scraped out.

'Coloured vases on the table' (boy, 12). For technique, see p. 23.

Wax scraper technique. 'Dark faces' (boys, 10). For technique, see pp. 23 and 25.

'The pheasant' (girl, 11). Scraper technique. For technique, see p. 23.

'Big red goldfish' (girl, 12). Wax crayon etching. For technique, see p. 26.

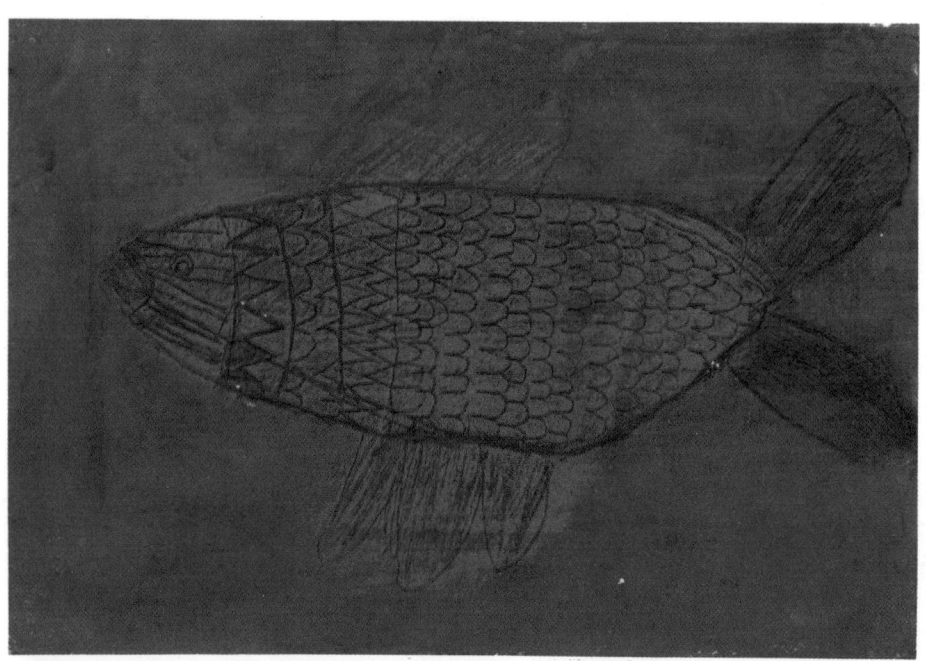

Nature study. 'Branches of Scots pine'. Underpainting in white wax crayon. Overpainting with coloured tempera, afterwards scraped out. For technique, see p. 23.

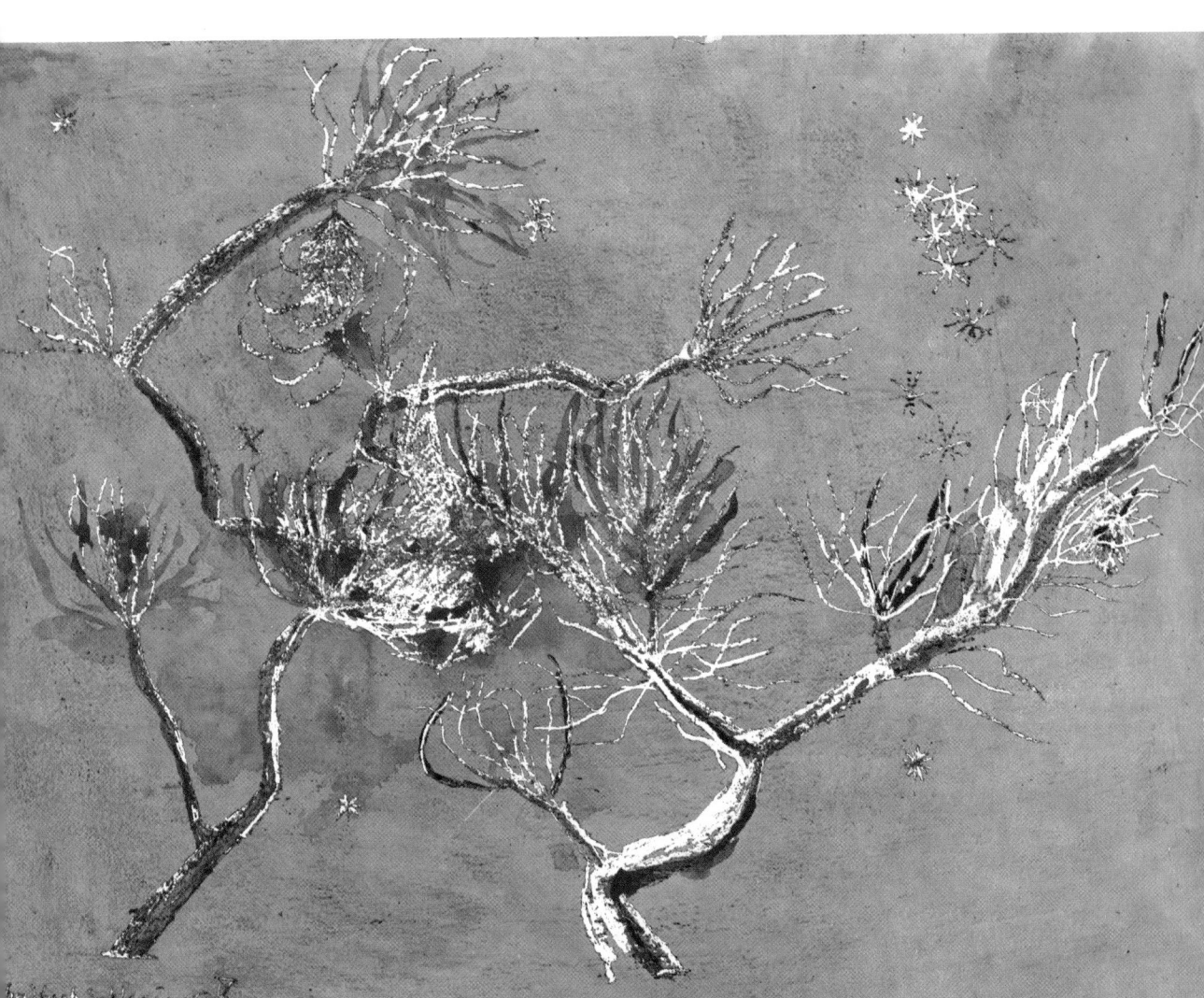

'The fisherman,' Drawing by a girl of 8, using wax crayons and opaque paint.

'The sorcerer strides through the land in seven-league boots.' For technique, see p. 27.

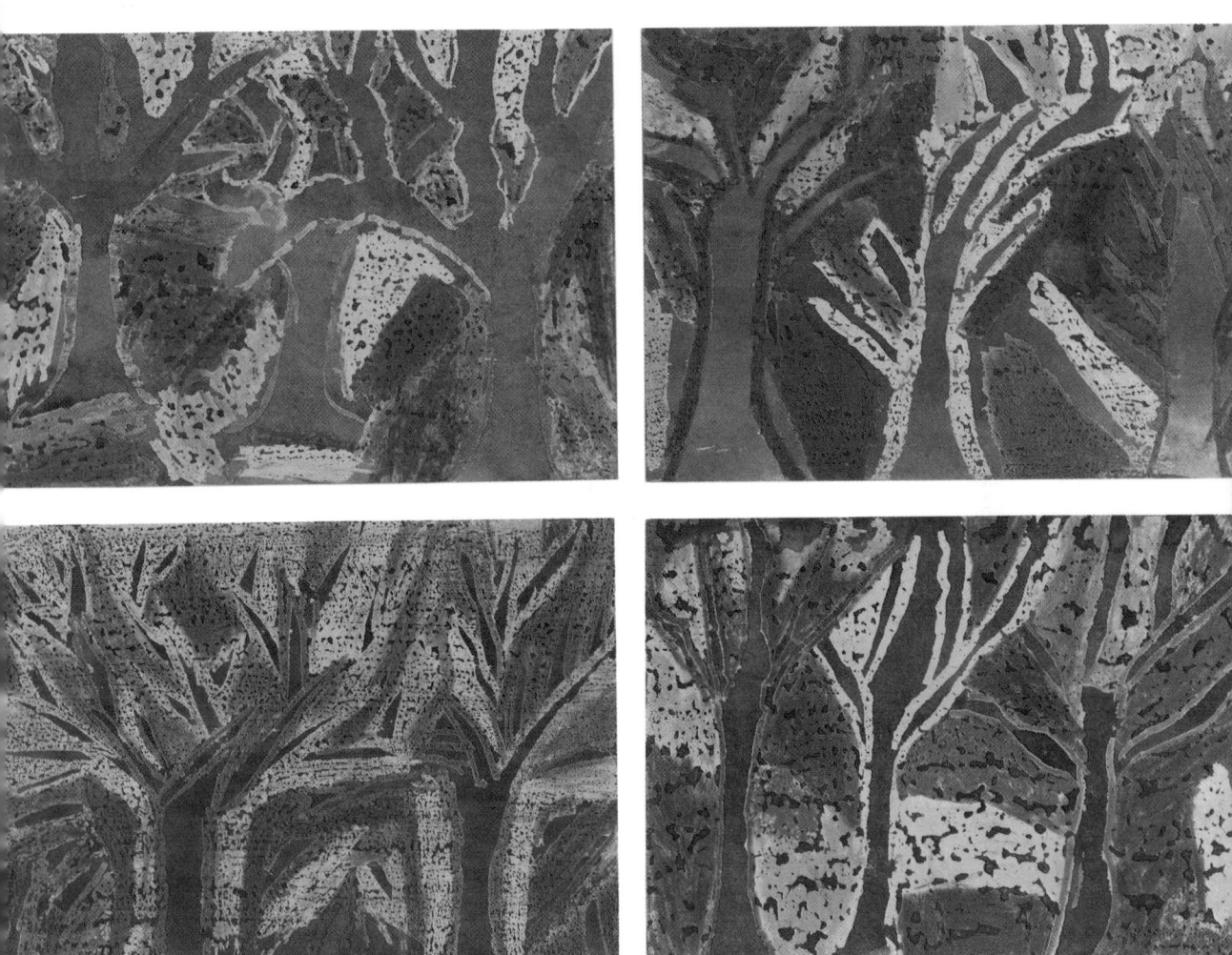

The trees were left white on a coloured ground. Then dark water-colour was swept over the whole with rapid strokes of the brush. The white trees soaked up the colour (boys, 10). For technique, see p. 27.

67

'Summer flowers in a bowl.' The
wax crayon was 'worked over'
with paintbrush and turpentine.
For technique, see p. 30.

'Woodland.' Painted with wax
crayon, and then worked over
with a rag dipped in turpentine.
For technique, see p. 30.

69

Here we have the multicoloured 'transfer printing' process. (see p. 36). This produces delicate pictures of a pastel character.

The theme was 'The roosters run a race over the meadow'. Of course this is something of a technical game, but a lot can be learnt from it, which will be of use later on, when printing from multicoloured lino blocks.

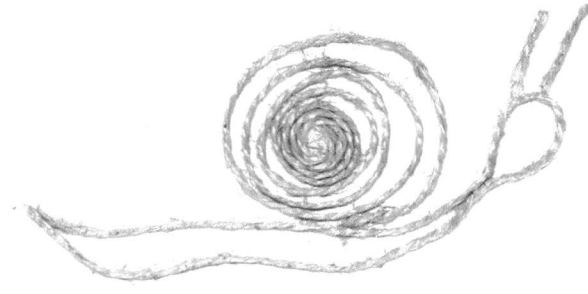

In her first school year Marita pasted this snail made of string on to a firm surface, and then laid a piece of drawing paper over it and made a rubbing with a wax crayon. She then rubbed several snails beside and over one another, using a different colour for each. For technique, see p. 37.

Marita

Another process is an adaptation of the lino print.

Take a finished lino-cut, apply thoroughly dampened, thick, drawing paper and press down with the thumb. This produces a paper relief, fitting the shapes of the lino-cut. When this is dry, it can be treated as a transfer. Its particular attractiveness consists in the possibility of 'printing' from it in several colours at once.

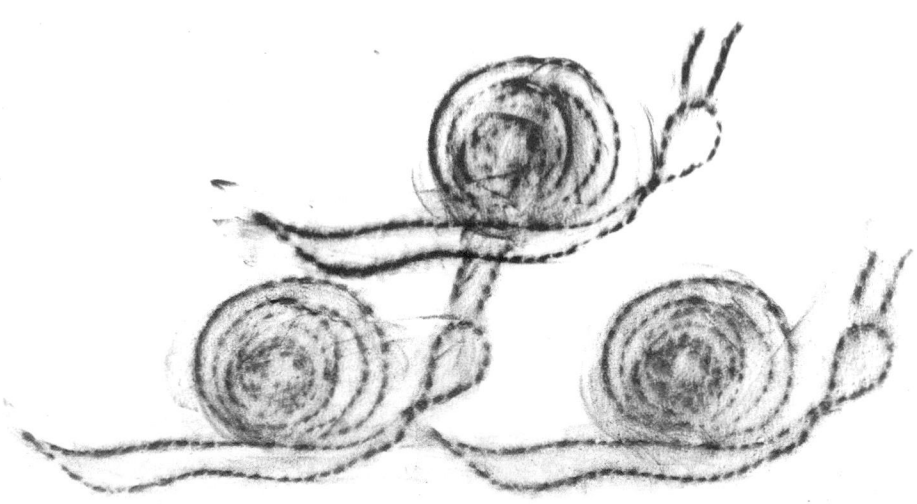

Colour clash and harmony.

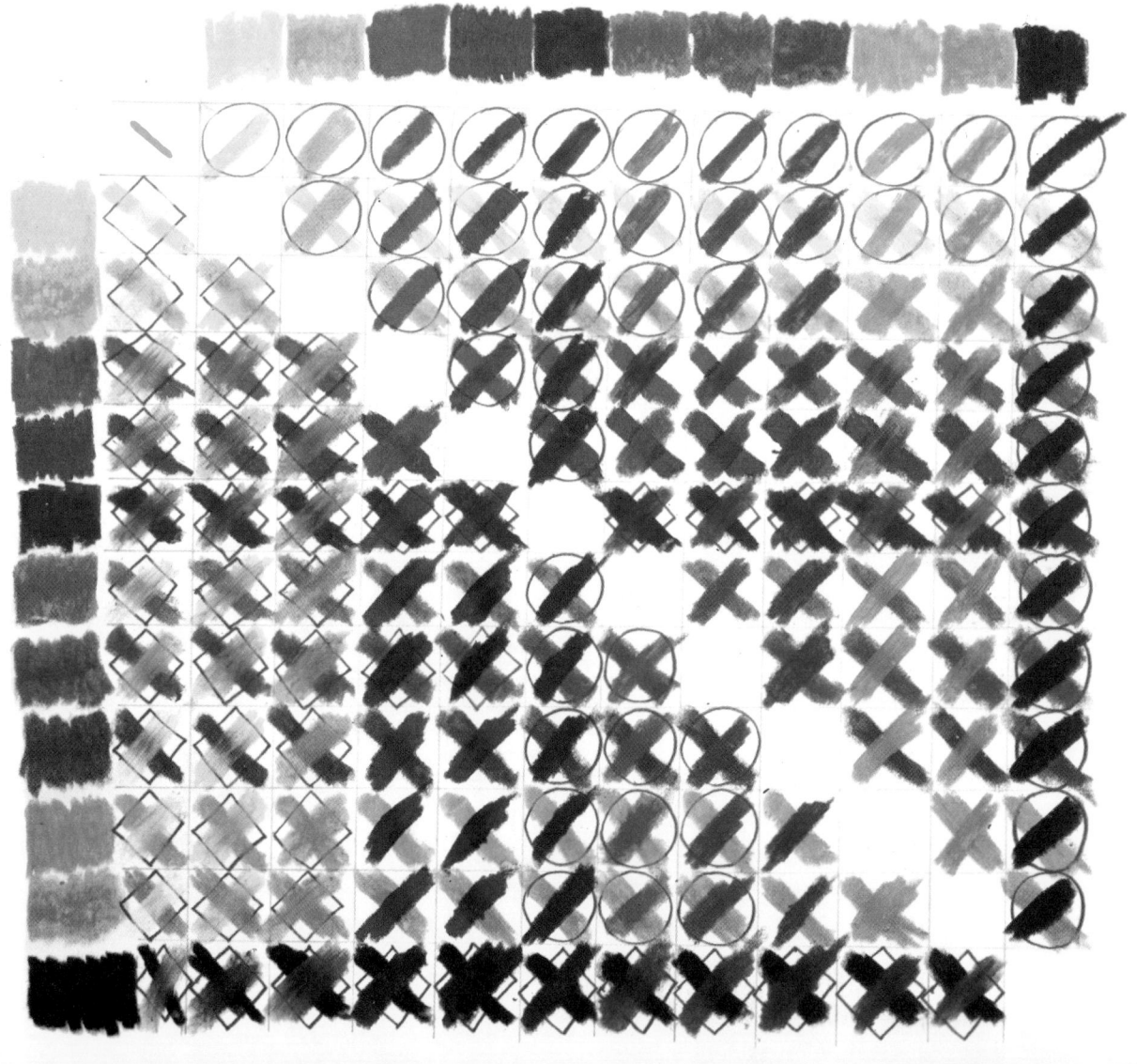

The basic colouring matter is consolidated by the wax, so it will not powder off or smear, but of course it must not be allowed to get too hot. The colours can be mixed, provided the lighter, harder ones are applied over the softer, darker ones. Dark over light lets nothing through. Wax is soluble in turpentine, benzine and other volatile solvents, and unwanted traces of colour can be removed by any of these. But soap and water are also efficient.

A typical scraper, with which light colours that have been covered over with dark ones can be scratched out again (see p. 20). The crumbs of wax resulting from this should be removed at intervals, before they fall on the floor and cause damaging stains.

Index

Table of Technical Skill Levels for Grades 1 through 9

There are simple, difficult, and genuinely complex techniques in drawing with wax crayons. Not all of these are equally suited to all age groups. Yet, it is often amazing to see the fine results obtained by younger children when they have received proper guidance and have been thoroughly familiarized with the techniques at an early stage.

The following table is merely intended to serve as a helpful guide in determining which techniques can be offered at each age level with the greatest probability, under correct guidance, of useful results and more success. The series of numbers refer to the pages.

Grade	1:	8, 13, 20, 25, (39 with proper guidance)
Grade	2:	8, 9, 13, 20, 25, (37 possibly), 39
Grade	3:	9, 10, 11, 13, 14, 15, 20, 25, 27, 34 top, 37, 39
Grade	4:	9, 10, 11, 12 bottom, 13, 14, 15, 17, 20, 22 top, 25, 26, 27, 30 bottom, 34 top, 37, 39
Grade	5:	10, 11, 12 bottom, 13, 14, 15, 17, 20, 21 top, 22 top, 24, 25, 26, 27, 29, 30 bottom, 33 bottom, 34, 35, 37, 39
Grade	6:	10, 11, 12 bottom, 13, 14, 15, 17, 20, 21 top, 22 top, 23, 24, 25, 26, 27, 29, 30 bottom, 33 bottom, 34, 35, 36, 37, 39
Grades 7, 8 and	9:	10, 11, 12 bottom, 13, 14, 15, 17, 18, 20, 21 top, 22 top, 23, 24, 25, 26, 27, 29, 30 top, 30 bottom, 32, 33, 34, 35, 36, 37, 39, 40, 41, 42